ON SOME OF LIFE'S IDEALS

ON A CERTAIN BLINDNESS IN HUMAN BEINGS ∴ ∴ WHAT MAKES A LIFE SIGNIFICANT

BY

WILLIAM JAMES

Martino Fine Books
Eastford, CT 06242
2016

Martino Fine Books
P.O. Box 913,
Eastford, CT 06242 USA

ISBN 978-1-68422-030-4

© *2016 Martino Fine Books*

Cover Design Tiziana Matarazzo

Printed in the United States of America On 100% Acid-Free Paper

ON SOME OF LIFE'S IDEALS

ON A CERTAIN BLINDNESS IN HUMAN BEINGS ∴ ∴ WHAT MAKES A LIFE SIGNIFICANT

BY

WILLIAM JAMES

NEW YORK
HENRY HOLT AND COMPANY

BY WILLIAM JAMES

The Principles of Psychology. 2 vols. 8vo. $5.00 *Edcl. net.* New York: Henry Holt & Co. 1890.

Psychology: Briefer course. 12mo. $1.60 *Edcl. net.* New York: Henry Holt & Co. 1892.

The Varieties of Religious Experience. $3.20 *net.* New York: Longmans, Green, & Co. 1902.

The Will to Believe, and Other Essays in Popular Philosophy. 12mo. $2.00. New York: Longmans, Green, & Co. 1897.

Is Life Worth Living? 18mo. 50 cents *net.* Philadelphia: S. B. Weston, 1305 Arch Street. 1896.

Human Immortality: Two supposed Objections to the Doctrine. 16mo. $1.00. Boston: Houghton, Mifflin & Co. 1898.

Pragmatism. $1.25 *net.* New York: Longmans, Green, & Co. 1907.

The Meaning of Truth: A Sequel to Pragmatism. $1.25 *net.* New York: Longmans, Green, & Co. 1909.

A Pluralistic Universe. $1.50 *net.* New York: Longmans, Green, & Co. 1909.

Memories and Studies. $1.75 *net.* New York: Longmans, Green, & Co. 1911.

Some Problems in Philosophy. $1.25 *net.* New York: Longmans, Green, & Co. 1911.

Essays in Radical Empiricism. $1.25 *net.* New York: Longmans, Green, & Co. 1912.

On Some of Life's Ideals. "On a Certain Blindness in Human Beings" and "What Makes a Life Significant." Reprinted from *Talks to Teachers.* 16mo. 50 cents *net.* New York: Henry Holt & Co. 1912.

Habit. Reprinted from *The Principles of Psychology.* 16mo. 50 cents *net.* New York: Henry Holt & Co. 1914.

On Vital Reserves. "The Energies of Men," from *Memories and Studies* and "The Gospel of Relaxation" from *Talks to Teachers.* 16mo. 50 cents *net.* New York: Henry Holt & Co. 1916.

The Literary Remains of Henry James. Edited, with an introduction, by WILLIAM JAMES. With Portrait. Crown 8vo. $2.00. Boston: Houghton, Mifflin & Co. 1885.

Talks to Teachers on Psychology: and to Students on Some of Life's Ideals. The complete book, from which the two essays contained in the present volume are reprinted. 12mo. $1.50 *Edcl. net.* New York: Henry Holt & Co. 1899.

ON A CERTAIN BLINDNESS IN HUMAN BEINGS

ON
A CERTAIN BLINDNESS
IN HUMAN BEINGS

OUR judgments concerning the worth of things, big or little, depend on the *feelings* the things arouse in us. Where we judge a thing to be precious in consequence of the *idea* we frame of it, this is only because the idea is itself associated already with a feeling. If we were radically feelingless, and if ideas were the only things our mind could entertain, we should lose all our likes and dislikes at a stroke, and be unable to point to any one situation or experience in life more valuable or significant than any other.

Now the blindness in human beings, of which this discourse will treat, is the blindness with which we all are afflicted in regard to the feelings of creatures and people different from ourselves.

[3]

We are practical beings, each of us with limited functions and duties to perform. Each is bound to feel intensely the importance of his own duties and the significance of the situations that call these forth. But this feeling is in each of us a vital secret, for sympathy with which we vainly look to others. The others are too much absorbed in their own vital secrets to take an interest in ours. Hence the stupidity and injustice of our opinions, so far as they deal with the significance of alien lives. Hence the falsity of our judgments, so far as they presume to decide in an absolute way on the value of other persons' conditions or ideals.

Take our dogs and ourselves, connected as we are by a tie more intimate than most ties in this world; and yet, outside of that tie of friendly fondness, how insensible, each of us, to all that makes life significant for the other! — we to the rapture of bones under hedges, or smells of trees and lamp-posts, they to the delights of literature and art. As you sit reading the most moving romance you ever fell upon, what sort of a judge is your fox-terrier of your behavior? With all his good will toward you, the nature of your conduct is absolutely excluded from his comprehension. To sit there like a senseless statue, when you might be taking him to walk and throwing sticks for him to catch! What queer disease is this that comes over you every day, of holding things and staring at them like that for hours together, paralyzed of motion and vacant of all conscious life? The African savages came nearer the truth; but they, too, missed it, when they gathered wonderingly round one of our American travellers who, in the interior, had just come into possession of a stray copy of the New York *Commercial Advertiser*, and was devouring it column by column. When he got through, they offered him a high price for the mysterious object; and, being asked for what they wanted it, they said: "For an eye medicine,"—that being the only reason they could conceive of for the protracted bath which he had given his eyes upon its surface.

The spectator's judgment is sure to miss the root of the matter, and to possess no truth. The subject judged knows a part of the world of reality which the judging spectator fails to see, knows more while the spectator knows less; and, wherever there is conflict of opinion and difference of vision, we are bound to believe that the truer side is the side that feels the more, and not the side that feels the less.

Let me take a personal example of the kind that befalls each one of us daily: —

Some years ago, while journeying in the mountains of North Carolina, I passed by a large number of 'coves,' as they call them there, or heads of small valleys between the hills, which had been newly cleared and planted. The impression on my mind was one of unmitigated squalor. The settler had in every case cut down the more manageable trees, and left their charred stumps standing. The larger trees he had girdled and killed, in order that their foliage should not cast a shade. He had then built a log cabin, plastering its chinks with clay, and had set up a tall zigzag rail fence around the scene of his havoc, to keep the pigs and cattle out. Finally, he had irregularly planted the intervals between the stumps and trees with Indian corn, which grew among the chips; and there he dwelt with his wife and babes — an axe, a gun, a few utensils, and some pigs and chickens feeding in the woods, being the sum total of his possessions.

The forest had been destroyed; and what had 'improved' it out of existence was hideous, a sort of ulcer, without a single element of artificial grace to make up for the loss of Nature's beauty. Ugly, indeed, seemed the life of the squatter, scudding, as the sailors say, under bare poles, beginning again away back where our first ancestors started, and by hardly a single item the better off for all the achievements of the intervening generations.

Talk about going back to nature! I said to myself, oppressed by the dreariness, as I drove by. Talk of a country life for one's old age and for one's children! Never thus, with nothing but the bare ground and one's bare hands to fight the battle! Never, without the best spoils of culture woven in! The beauties and commodities gained by the centuries are sacred. They are our heritage and birthright. No modern person ought to be willing to live a day in such a state of rudimentariness and <u>denudation</u>.

Then I said to the mountaineer who was driving me, " What sort of people are they who have to make these new clearings? " " All of us," he replied. " Why, we ain't happy here, unless we are getting one of these coves under cultivation." I instantly felt that I had been losing the whole inward significance of the situation. Because to me the clearings spoke of naught but denudation, I thought that to those whose sturdy arms and obedient axes had made them they could tell no other story. But, when *they*

looked on the hideous stumps, what they
thought of was personal victory. The chips,
the girdled trees, and the vile split rails
spoke of honest sweat, persistent toil, and
final reward. The cabin was a warrant of
safety for self and wife and babes. In
short, the clearing, which to me was a mere
ugly picture on the retina, was to them a
symbol redolent with moral memories and
sang a very pæan of duty, struggle, and
success.

I had been as blind to the peculiar ideality of their conditions as they certainly
would also have been to the ideality of
mine, had they had a peep at my strange
indoor academic ways of life at Cambridge.

Wherever a process of life communicates
an eagerness to him who lives it, there the
life becomes genuinely significant. Sometimes the eagerness is more knit up with the
motor activities, sometimes with the per-
ceptions, sometimes with the imagination,
sometimes with reflective thought. But,

wherever it is found, there is the zest, the tingle, the excitement of reality; and there *is* 'importance' in the only real and positive sense in which importance ever anywhere can be.

Robert Louis Stevenson has illustrated this by a case, drawn from the sphere of the imagination, in an essay which I really think deserves to become immortal, both for the truth of its matter and the excellence of its form.

"Toward the end of September," Stevenson writes, "when school-time was drawing near, and the nights were already black, we would begin to sally from our respective villas, each equipped with a tin bull's-eye lantern. The thing was so well known that it had worn a rut in the commerce of Great Britain; and the grocers, about the due time, began to garnish their windows with our particular brand of luminary. We wore them buckled to the waist upon a cricket belt, and over them, such was the rigor of the game, a buttoned top-coat.

They smelled noisomely of blistered tin.
They never burned aright, though they
would always burn our fingers. Their use
was naught, the pleasure of them merely
fanciful, and yet a boy with a bull's-eye
under his top-coat asked for nothing more.
The fishermen used lanterns about their
boats, and it was from them, I suppose, that
we had got the hint; but theirs were not
bull's-eyes, nor did we ever play at being
fishermen. The police carried them at their
belts, and we had plainly copied them in
that; yet we did not pretend to be policemen. Burglars, indeed, we may have had
some haunting thought of; and we had certainly an eye to past ages when lanterns
were more common, and to certain story-
books in which we had found them to figure
very largely. But take it for all in all, the
pleasure of the thing was substantive; and
to be a boy with a bull's-eye under his
topcoat was good enough for us.

"When two of these asses met, there
would be an anxious 'Have you got your

lantern?' and a gratified 'Yes!' That was
the shibboleth, and very needful, too; for,
as it was the rule to keep our glory contained,
none could recognize a lantern-bearer unless
(like the polecat) by the smell. Four or
five would sometimes climb into the belly
of a ten-man lugger, with nothing but the
thwarts above them,—for the cabin was
usually locked,—or choose out some hollow
of the links where the wind might whistle
overhead. Then the coats would be unbut-
toned, and the bull's-eyes discovered; and
in the chequering glimmer, under the huge,
windy hall of the night, and cheered by a
rich steam of toasting tinware, these fortunate young gentlemen would crouch together in the cold sand of the links, or on
the scaly bilges of the fishing-boat, and delight them with inappropriate talk. Woe
is me that I cannot give some specimens!
. . . But the talk was but a condiment,
and these gatherings themselves only acci-
dents in the career of the lantern-bearer.
The essence of this bliss was to walk by

yourself in the black night, the slide shut, the top-coat buttoned, not a ray escaping, whether to conduct your footsteps or to make your glory public,—a mere pillar of darkness in the dark; and all the while, deep down in the privacy of your fool's heart, to know you had a bull's-eye at your belt, and to exult and sing over the knowledge.

"It is said that a poet has died young in the breast of the most stolid. It may be contended rather that a (somewhat minor) bard in almost every case survives, and is the spice of life to his possessor. Justice is not done to the versatility and the un-plumbed childishness of man's imagination. His life from without may seem but a rude mound of mud: there will be some golden chamber at the heart of it, in which he dwells delighted; and for as dark as his pathway seems to the observer, he will have some kind of bull's-eye at his belt.

. . . "There is one fable that touches very near the quick of life,—the fable of the monk who passed into the woods, heard a bird break into song, hearkened for a trill or two, and found himself at his return a stranger at his convent gates; for he had been absent fifty years, and of all his comrades there survived but one to recognize him. It is not only in the woods that this enchanter carols, though perhaps he is native there. He sings in the most doleful places. The miser hears him and chuckles, and his days are moments. With no more apparatus than an evil-smelling lantern, I have evoked him on the naked links. All life that is not merely mechanical is spun out of two strands, —seeking for that bird and hearing him. And it is just this that makes life so hard to value, and the delight of each so incommunicable. And it is just a knowledge of this, and a remembrance of those fortunate hours in which the bird *has* sung to *us*, that fills us with such wonder when we turn to the pages of the realist. There, to be sure, we find a picture of life in so far as it consists of mud and of old iron, cheap desires and cheap fears, that which we are ashamed to remember and that which we are careless whether we forget; but of the note of that time-devouring nightingale we hear no news.

. . . "Say that we came [in such a realistic romance] on some such business as that of my lantern-bearers on the links, and described the boys as very cold, spat upon by flurries of rain, and drearily surrounded, all of which they were; and their talk as silly and indecent, which it certainly was. To the eye of the observer they *are* wet and cold and drearily surrounded; but ask themselves, and they are in the heaven of a recondite pleasure, the ground of which is an ill-smelling lantern.

"For, to repeat, the ground of a man's joy is often hard to hit. It may hinge at times upon a mere accessory, like the lantern; it may reside in the mysterious inwards of psychology. . . . It has so little bond with externals . . . that it may even touch them not, and the man's true life, for which he consents to live, lie together in the field of fancy. . . . In such a case the poetry runs underground. The observer (poor soul, with his documents!) is all abroad. For to look at the man is but to court deception. We shall see the trunk from which he draws his nourishment; but he himself is above and abroad in the green dome of foliage, hummed through by winds and nested in by nightingales. And the true realism were that of the poets, to climb after him like a squirrel, and catch some glimpse of the heaven in which he lives. And the true realism, always and everywhere, is that of the poets: to find out where joy resides, and give it a voice far beyond singing.

"For to miss the joy is to miss all. In the joy of the actors lies the sense of any action. That is the explanation, that the excuse. To one who has not the secret of the lanterns the scene upon the links is meaningless. And hence the haunting and truly spectral unreality of realistic books.

. . . In each we miss the personal poetry, the enchanted atmosphere, that rainbow work of fancy that clothes what is naked and seems to ennoble what is base; in each, life falls dead like dough, instead of soaring away like a balloon into the colors of the sunset; each is true, each inconceivable; for no man lives in the external truth among salts and acids, but in the warm, phantasmagoric chamber of his brain, with the painted windows and the storied wall." [1]

These paragraphs are the best thing I know in all Stevenson. "To miss the joy is to miss all." Indeed, it is. Yet we are but finite, and each one of us has some single specialized vocation of his own. And it seems as if energy in the service of its particular duties might be got only by hardening the heart toward everything unlike them. Our deadness toward all but one particular kind of joy would thus be

[1] 'The Lantern-bearers,' in the volume entitled 'Across the Plains.' Abridged in the quotation.

the price we inevitably have to pay for being practical creatures. Only in some pitiful dreamer, some philosopher, poet, or romancer, or when the common practical man becomes a lover, does the hard externality give way, and a gleam of insight into the ejective world, as Clifford called it, the vast world of inner life beyond us, so different from that of outer seeming, illuminate our mind. Then the whole scheme of our customary values gets confounded, then our self is riven and its narrow interests fly to pieces, then a new centre and a new perspective must be found.

The change is well described by my colleague, Josiah Royce: —

"What, then, is our neighbor? Thou hast regarded his thought, his feeling, as somehow different from thine. Thou hast said, 'A pain in him is not like a pain in me, but something far easier to bear.' He seems to thee a little less living than thou; his life is dim, it is cold, it is a pale fire beside thy own burning desires. . . . So, dimly and

by instinct hast thou lived with thy neighbor, and hast known him not, being blind.
Thou hast made [of him] a thing, no Self
at all. Have done with this illusion, and
simply try to learn the truth. Pain is pain,
joy is joy, everywhere, even as in thee.
In all the songs of the forest birds; in all
the cries of the wounded and dying,
struggling in the captor's power; in the
boundless sea where the myriads of water-
creatures strive and die; amid all the countless hordes of savage men; in all sickness and
sorrow; in all exultation and hope, everywhere, from the lowest to the noblest, the
same conscious, burning, wilful life is found,
endlessly manifold as the forms of the living creatures, unquenchable as the fires of
the sun, real as these impulses that even now
throb in thine own little selfish heart. Lift
up thy eyes, behold that life, and then turn
away, and forget it as thou canst; but, if
thou hast *known* that, thou hast begun to
know thy duty." [1]

[1] The Religious Aspect of Philosophy, pp. 157–162 (abridged).

This higher vision of an inner significance in what, until then, we had realized only in the dead external way, often comes over a person suddenly; and, when it does so, it makes an epoch in his history. As Emerson says, there is a depth in those moments that constrains us to ascribe more reality to them than to all other experiences. The passion of love will shake one like an explosion, or some act will awaken a remorseful compunction that hangs like a cloud over all one's later day.

This mystic sense of hidden meaning starts upon us often from non-human natural things. I take this passage from 'Obermann,' a French novel that had some vogue in its day: "Paris, March 7.— It was dark and rather cold. I was gloomy, and walked because I had nothing to do. I passed by some flowers placed breast-high upon a wall. A jonquil in bloom was there. It is the strongest expression of desire: it was the first perfume of the year. I felt all the happiness destined for man. This unutterable

harmony of souls, the phantom of the ideal
world, arose in me complete. I never felt
anything so great or so instantaneous. I
know not what shape, what analogy, what
secret of relation it was that made me see in
this flower a limitless beauty. . . . I shall
never enclose in a conception this power,
this immensity that nothing will express;
this form that nothing will contain; this ideal
of a better world which one feels, but which
it would seem that nature has not made." [1]

Wordsworth and Shelley are similarly
full of this sense of a limitless significance
in natural things. In Wordsworth it was
a somewhat austere and moral significance,
— a 'lonely cheer.'

> To every natural form, rock, fruit, or flower,
> Even the loose stones that cover the highway,
> I gave a moral life: I saw them feel
> Or linked them to some feeling: the great mass
> Lay bedded in some quickening soul, and all
> That I beheld respired with inward meaning.[2]

[1] De Sénancour: Obermann, Lettre XXX.
[2] The Prelude, Book III.

"Authentic tidings of invisible things!"
Just what this hidden presence in nature
was, which Wordsworth so rapturously felt,
and in the light of which he lived, tramping
the hills for days together, the poet never
could explain logically or in articulate
conceptions. Yet to the reader who may
himself have had gleaming moments of a
similar sort the verses in which Wordsworth simply proclaims the fact of them
come with a heart-satisfying authority: —

                        Magnificent
The morning rose, in memorable pomp,
Glorious as ere I had beheld.   In front
The sea lay laughing at a distance; near
The solid mountains shone, bright as the clouds,
Grain-tinctured, drenched in empyrean light;
And in the meadows and the lower grounds
Was all the sweetness of a common dawn,—
Dews, vapors, and the melody of birds,
And laborers going forth to till the fields.

Ah! need I say, dear Friend, that to the brim
My heart was full; I made no vows, but vows
Were then made for me; bond unknown to me

Was given, that I should be, else sinning greatly,
A dedicated Spirit.   On I walked,
In thankful blessedness, which yet survives.[1]

As Wordsworth walked, filled with this strange inner joy, responsive thus to the secret life of nature round about him, his rural neighbors, tightly and narrowly intent upon their own affairs, their crops and lambs and fences, must have thought him a very insignificant and foolish personage. It surely never occurred to any one of them to wonder what was going on inside of *him* or what it might be worth.   And yet that inner life of his carried the burden of a significance that has fed the souls of others, and fills them to this day with inner joy.

Richard Jefferies has written a remarkable autobiographic document entitled, 'The Story of my Heart.'   It tells, in many pages, of the rapture with which in youth the sense of the life of nature filled him.   On a certain hill-top he says: —

[1] The Prelude, Book IV.

"I was utterly alone with the sun and the earth. Lying down on the grass, I spoke in my soul to the earth, the sun, the air, and the distant sea, far beyond sight. . . . With all the intensity of feeling which exalted me, all the intense communion I held with the earth, the sun and sky, the stars hidden by the light, with the ocean, — in no manner can the thrilling depth of these feelings be written, — with these I prayed as if they were the keys of an instrument. . . . The great sun, burning with light, the strong earth, — dear earth, — the warm sky, the pure air, the thought of ocean, the inexpressible beauty of all filled me with a rapture, an ecstasy, an inflatus. With this inflatus, too, I prayed. . . . The prayer, this soul-emotion, was in itself, not for an object: it was a passion. I hid my face in the grass. I was wholly prostrated, I lost myself in the wrestle, I was rapt and carried away. . . . Had any shepherd accidentally seen me lying on the turf, he would only have thought I was resting a few minutes.

I made no outward show. Who could have imagined the whirlwind of passion that was going on in me as I reclined there!"[1]

Surely, a worthless hour of life, when measured by the usual standards of commercial value. Yet in what other *kind* of value can the preciousness of any hour, made precious by any standard, consist, if it consist not in feelings of excited significance like these, engendered in some one, by what the hour contains?

Yet so blind and dead does the clamor of our own practical interests make us to all other things, that it seems almost as if it were necessary to become worthless as a practical being, if one is to hope to attain to any breadth of insight into the impersonal world of worths as such, to have any perception of life's meaning on a large objective scale. Only your mystic, your dreamer, or your insolvent tramp or loafer, can afford so sympathetic an occupation, an occupation which will change the usual standards of

[1] *Op. cit.*, Boston, Roberts, 1883, pp. 5, 6.

human value in the twinkling of an eye,
giving to foolishness a place ahead of power,
and laying low in a minute the distinctions
which it takes a hard-working conventional
man a lifetime to build up. You may be a
prophet, at this rate; but you cannot be
a worldly success.

Walt Whitman, for instance, is accounted
by many of us a contemporary prophet.
He abolishes the usual human distinctions,
brings all conventionalisms into solution,
and loves and celebrates hardly any human
attributes save those elementary ones common to all members of the race. For this
he becomes a sort of ideal tramp, a rider on
omnibus-tops and ferry-boats, and, considered either practically or academically, a
worthless, unproductive being. His verses
are but ejaculations—things mostly without subject or verb, a succession of inter-
jections on an immense scale. He felt the
human crowd as rapturously as Wordsworth
felt the mountains, felt it as an overpower-
ingly significant presence, simply to absorb

one's mind in which should be business sufficient and worthy to fill the days of a serious man.   As he crosses Brooklyn ferry, this is what he feels: —

Flood-tide below me!   I watch you, face to face;
Clouds of the west! sun there half an hour high!
   I see you also face to face.
Crowds of men and women attired in the usual
   costumes! how curious you are to me!
On the ferry-boats, the hundreds and hundreds that
   cross, returning home, are more curious to me
   than you suppose;
And you that shall cross from shore to shore years
   hence, are more to me, and more in my medi-
   tations, than you might suppose.
Others will enter the gates of the ferry, and cross
   from shore to shore;
Others will watch the run of the flood-tide;
Others will see the shipping of Manhattan north
   and west, and the heights of Brooklyn to the
   south and east;
Others will see the islands large and small;
Fifty years hence, others will see them as they cross,
   the sun half an hour high.
A hundred years hence, or ever so many hundred
   years hence, others will see them,

Will enjoy the sunset, the pouring in of the flood-
tide, the falling back to the sea of the ebb-tide.
It avails not, neither time or place — distance avails
not.
Just as you feel when you look on the river and sky,
so I felt;
Just as any of you is one of a living crowd, I was
one of a crowd;
Just as you are refresh'd by the gladness of the river
and the bright flow, I was refresh'd;
Just as you stand and lean on the rail, yet hurry
with the swift current, I stood, yet was hurried;
Just as you look on the numberless masts of ships,
and the thick-stemmed pipes of steamboats, I
looked.
I too many and many a time cross'd the river,
the sun half an hour high;
I watched the Twelfth-month sea-gulls — I saw
them high in the air, with motionless wings,
oscillating their bodies,
I saw how the glistening yellow lit up parts of their
bodies, and left the rest in strong shadow,
I saw the slow-wheeling circles, and the gradual
edging toward the south.
Saw the white sails of schooners and sloops, saw
the ships at anchor,
The sailors at work in the rigging, or out astride
the spars;

The scallop-edged waves in the twilight, the ladled
    cups, the frolicsome crests and glistening;
The stretch afar growing dimmer and dimmer, the
    gray walls of the granite store-houses by the
    docks;
On the neighboring shores, the fires from the foun-
    dry chimneys burning high . . . into the night,
Casting their flicker of black . . . into the clefts
    of streets.
These, and all else, were to me the same as they are
    to you.[1]

And so on, through the rest of a divinely
beautiful poem. And, if you wish to see
what this hoary loafer considered the most
worthy way of profiting by life's heaven-
sent opportunities, read the delicious volume
of his letters to a young car-conductor who
had become his friend:—

                "New York, Oct. 9, 1868.

   "*Dear Pete,* — It is splendid here this
forenoon — bright and cool. I was out
early taking a short walk by the river only
two squares from where I live. . . . Shall I

[1] Crossing Brooklyn Ferry (abridged).

tell you about [my life] just to fill up? I generally spend the forenoon in my room writing, etc., then take a bath fix up and go out about twelve and loafe somewhere or call on someone down town or on business, or perhaps if it is very pleasant and I feel like it ride a trip with some driver friend on Broadway from 23rd Street to Bowling Green, three miles each way. (Every day I find I have plenty to do, every hour is occupied with something.) You know it is a never ending amusement and study and recreation for me to ride a couple of hours on a pleasant afternoon on a Broadway stage in this way. You see everything as you pass, a sort of living, endless panorama —shops and splendid buildings and great windows: on the broad sidewalks crowds of women richly dressed continually passing, altogether different, superior in style and looks from any to be seen anywhere else —in fact a perfect stream of people —men too dressed in high style, and plenty of foreigners— and then in the streets the thick crowd of

carriages, stages, carts, hotel and private
coaches, and in fact all sorts of vehicles and
many first class teams, mile after mile, and
the splendor of such a great street and so
many tall, ornamental, noble buildings many
of them of white marble, and the gayety
and motion on every side: you will not
wonder how much attraction all this is on
a fine day, to a great loafer like me, who
enjoys so much seeing the busy world move
by him, and exhibiting itself for his amusement, while he takes it easy and just looks
on and observes." [1]

Truly a futile way of passing the time,
some of you may say, and not altogether
creditable to a grown-up man. And yet,
from the deepest point of view, who knows
the more of truth, and who knows the less,
—Whitman on his omnibus-top, full of
the inner joy with which the spectacle
inspires him, or you, full of the dis-
dain which the futility of his occupation
excites?

[1] Calamus, Boston, 1897, pp. 41, 42.

When your ordinary Brooklynite or New York, leading a life replete with too much luxury, or tired and careworn about his personal affairs, crosses the ferry or goes up Broadway, *his* fancy does not thus 'soar away into the colors of the sunset' as did Whitman's, nor does he inwardly realize at all the indisputable fact that this world never did anywhere or at any time contain more of essential divinity, or of eternal meaning, than is embodied in the fields of vision over which his eyes so carelessly pass. There is life; and there, a step away, is death. There is the only kind of beauty there ever was. There is the old human struggle and its fruits together. There is the text and the sermon, the real and the ideal in one. But to the jaded and unquickened eye it is all dead and common, pure vulgarism, flatness, and disgust. "Hech! it is a sad sight!" says Carlyle, walking at night with some one who appeals to him to note the splendor of the stars. And that very repetition of the scene to new generations of men in *secula seculorum*, that eternal recurrence of the common order, which so fills a Whitman with mystic satisfaction, is to a Schopenhauer, with the emotional anæsthesia, the feeling of 'awful inner emptiness' from out of which he views it all, the chief ingredient of the tedium it instils.   What is life on the largest scale, he asks, but the same recurrent inanities, the same dog barking, the same fly buzzing, forevermore?   Yet of the kind of fibre of which such inanities consist is the material woven of all the excitements, joys, and meanings that ever were, or ever shall be, in this world.

To be rapt with satisfied attention, like Whitman, to the mere spectacle of the world's presence, is one way, and the most fundamental way, of confessing one's sense of its unfathomable significance and importance.   But how can one attain to the feeling of the vital significance of an experience, if one have it not to begin with?   There is no receipt which one can follow.   Being a secret and a mystery, it often comes in mysteriously unexpected ways. It blossoms sometimes from out of the very grave wherein we imagined that our happiness was buried. Benvenuto Cellini, after a life all in the outer sunshine, made of adventures and artistic excitements, suddenly finds himself cast into a dungeon in the Castle of San Angelo. The place is horrible. Rats and wet and mould possess it. His leg is broken and his teeth fall out, apparently with scurvy. But his thoughts turn to God as they have never turned before. He gets a Bible, which he reads during the one hour in the twenty-four in which a wandering ray of daylight penetrates his cavern. He has religious visions. He sings psalms to himself, and composes hymns. And thinking, on the last day of July, of the festivities customary on the morrow in Rome, he says to himself: "All these past years I celebrated this holiday with the vanities of the world: from this year henceforth I will do it with the divinity of God. And then I said to myself, 'Oh, how much more happy I am for this present life of mine than for all those things remembered!'"[1]

But the great understander of these mysterious ebbs and flows is Tolstoï. They throb all through his novels. In his 'War and Peace,' the hero, Peter, is supposed to be the richest man in the Russian empire. During the French invasion he is taken prisoner, and dragged through much of the retreat. Cold, vermin, hunger, and every form of misery assail him, the result being a revelation to him of the real scale of life's values. "Here only, and for the first time, he appreciated, because he was deprived of it, the happiness of eating when he was hungry, of drinking when he was thirsty, of sleeping when he was sleepy, and of talking when he felt the desire to exchange some words. . . . Later in life he always recurred with joy to this month of captivity, and never failed to speak with enthusiasm of the powerful and inefface-

[1] Vita, lib. 2, chap. iv.

able sensations, and especially of the moral calm which he had experienced at this epoch. When at daybreak, on the morrow of his imprisonment, he saw [I abridge here Tolstoï's description] the mountains with their wooded slopes disappearing in the gray- ish mist; when he felt the cool breeze caress him; when he saw the light drive away the vapors, and the sun rise majestically behind the clouds and cupolas, and the crosses, the dew, the distance, the river, sparkle in the splendid, cheerful rays,—his heart overflowed with emotion. This emotion kept continually with him, and increased a hundred-fold as the difficulties of his situa- tion grew graver. . . . He learnt that man is meant for happiness, and that this happi- ness is in him, in the satisfaction of the daily needs of existence, and that unhappiness is the fatal result, not of our need, but of our abundance. . . . When calm reigned in the camp, and the embers paled, and little by little went out, the full moon had reached the zenith. The woods and the fields roundabout lay clearly visible; and, beyond the inundation of light which filled them, the view plunged into the limitless horizon. Then Peter cast his eyes upon the firmament, filled at that hour with myriads of stars. 'All that is mine,' he thought. 'All that is in me, is me! And that is what they think they have taken prisoner! That is what they have shut up in a cabin!' So he smiled, and turned in to sleep among his comrades." [1]

The occasion and the experience, then, are nothing. It all depends on the capacity of the soul to be grasped, to have its life-currents absorbed by what is given. "Crossing a bare common," says Emerson, "in snow puddles, at twilight, under a clouded sky, without having in my thoughts any occurrence of special good fortune, I have enjoyed a perfect exhilaration. I am glad to the brink of fear."

Life is always worth living, if one have such responsive sensibilities. But we of the highly educated classes (so called)

[1] La Guerre et la Paix, Paris, 1884, vol. iii. pp. 268, 275, 316.

have most of us got far, far away from
Nature. We are trained to seek the choice,
the rare, the exquisite exclusively, and to
overlook the common. We are stuffed
with abstract conceptions, and glib with
verbalities and verbosities; and in the culture of these higher functions the peculiar
sources of joy connected with our simpler
functions often dry up, and we grow stone-
blind and insensible to life's more elementary and general goods and joys.

The remedy under such conditions is to
descend to a more profound and primitive
level. To be imprisoned or shipwrecked or
forced into the army would permanently
show the good of life to many an over-
educated pessimist. Living in the open
air and on the ground, the lop-sided beam of
the balance slowly rises to the level line;
and the over-sensibilities and insensibilities
even themselves out. The good of all the
artificial schemes and fevers fades and pales;
and that of seeing, smelling, tasting, sleeping, and daring and doing with one's body,

grows and grows. The savages and children of nature, to whom we deem ourselves
so much superior, certainly are alive where
we are often dead, along these lines; and,
could they write as glibly as we do, they
would read us impressive lectures on our
impatience for improvement and on our
blindness to the fundamental static goods
of life. "Ah! my brother," said a chief-
tain to his white guest, "thou wilt never
know the happiness of both thinking of
nothing and doing nothing. This, next to
sleep, is the most enchanting of all things.
Thus we were before our birth, and thus
we shall be after death. Thy people, . . .
when they have finished reaping one field,
they begin to plough another; and, if the
day were not enough, I have seen them
plough by moonlight. What is their life
to ours, — the life that is as naught to them?
Blind that they are, they lose it all! But
we live in the present." [1]

[1] Quoted by Lotze, Microcosmus, English translation, vol.
ii. p. 240.

The intense interest that life can assume
when brought down to the non-thinking
level, the level of pure sensorial perception,
has been beautifully described by a man
who *can* write, — Mr. W. H. Hudson, in
his volume, 'Idle Days in Patagonia.'

"I spent the greater part of one winter,"
says this admirable author, "at a point on
the Rio Negro, seventy or eighty miles from
the sea.

. . . "It was my custom to go out every
morning on horseback with my gun, and,
followed by one dog, to ride away from the
valley; and no sooner would I climb the
terrace, and plunge into the gray, universal
thicket, than I would find myself as completely alone as if five hundred instead of
only five miles separated me from the
valley and river.   So wild and solitary and
remote seemed that gray waste, stretching
away into infinitude, a waste untrodden
by man, and where the wild animals
are so few that they have made no
discoverable path in the wilderness of

thorns. . . . Not once nor twice nor thrice,
but day after day I returned to this soli-
tude, going to it in the morning as if to
attend a festival, and leaving it only when
hunger and thirst and the westering sun
compelled me. And yet I had no object
in going, — no motive which could be put
into words; for, although I carried a gun,
there was nothing to shoot, — the shoot-
ing was all left behind in the valley. . . .
Sometimes I would pass a whole day without seeing one mammal, and perhaps not more
than a dozen birds of any size. The weather
at that time was cheerless, generally with
a gray film of cloud spread over the sky,
and a bleak wind, often cold enough to make
my bridle-hand quite numb. . . . At a
slow pace, which would have seemed intol-
erable under other circumstances, I would
ride about for hours together at a stretch.
On arriving at a hill, I would slowly ride
to its summit, and stand there to survey
the prospect. On every side it stretched
away in great undulations, wild and irregu-

lar. How gray it all was! Hardly less so near at hand than on the haze-wrapped horizon where the hills were dim and the outline obscured by distance. Descending from my outlook, I would take up my aimless wanderings again, and visit other elevations to gaze on the same landscape from another point; and so on for hours. And at noon I would dismount, and sit or lie on my folded poncho for an hour or longer. One day in these rambles I discovered a small grove composed of twenty or thirty trees, growing at a convenient distance apart, that had evidently been resorted to by a herd of deer or other wild animals. This grove was on a hill differing in shape from other hills in its neighborhood; and, after a time, I made a point of finding and using it as a resting-place every day at noon. I did not ask myself why I made choice of that one spot, sometimes going out of my way to sit there, instead of sitting down under any one of the millions of trees and bushes on any other hillside.

I thought nothing about it, but acted unconsciously. Only afterward it seemed to me that, after having rested there once, each time I wished to rest again, the wish came associated with the image of that particular clump of trees, with polished stems and clean bed of sand beneath; and in a short time I formed a habit of returning, animal like, to repose at that same spot.

"It was, perhaps, a mistake to say that I would sit down and rest, since I was never tired; and yet, without being tired, that noon-day pause, during which I sat for an hour without moving, was strangely grateful. All day there would be no sound, not even the rustling of a leaf. One day, while *listening* to the silence, it occurred to my mind to wonder what the effect would be if I were to shout aloud. This seemed at the time a horrible suggestion, which almost made me shudder. But during those solitary days it was a rare thing for any thought to cross my mind. In the state of mind I was in, thought had become impossible. My state was one of *suspense* and *watchfulness;* yet I had no expectation of meeting an adventure, and felt as free from apprehension as I feel now while sitting in a room in London. The state seemed familiar rather than strange, and accompanied by a strong feeling of elation; and I did not know that something had come between me and my intellect until I returned to my former self, — to thinking, and the old insipid existence [again].

"I had undoubtedly *gone back;* and that state of intense watchfulness or alertness, rather, with suspension of the higher intellectual faculties, represented the mental state of the pure savage. He thinks little, reasons little, having a surer guide in his [mere sensory perceptions]. He is in perfect harmony with nature, and is nearly on a level, mentally, with the wild animals he preys on, and which in their turn sometimes prey on him." [1]

For the spectator, such hours as Mr.

[1] *Op. cit.*, pp. 210–222 (abridged).

Hudson writes of form a mere tale of emptiness, in which nothing happens, nothing is gained, and there is nothing to describe. They are meaningless and vacant tracts of time. To him who feels their inner secret, they tingle with an importance that unutterably vouches for itself. I am sorry for the boy or girl, or man or woman, who has never been touched by the spell of this mysterious sensorial life, with its irrationality, if so you like to call it, but its vigilance and its supreme felicity. The holidays of life are its most vitally significant portions, because they are, or at least should be, covered with just this kind of magically irresponsible spell.

And now what is the result of all these considerations and quotations? It is negative in one sense, but positive in another. It absolutely forbids us to be forward in pronouncing on the meaninglessness of forms of existence other than our own; and it commands us to tolerate, respect, and indulge those whom we see harmlessly interested and happy in their own ways, however unintelligible these may be to us. Hands off: neither the whole of truth nor the whole of good is revealed to any single observer, although each observer gains a partial superiority of insight from the peculiar position in which he stands. Even prisons and sick-rooms have their special revelations. It is enough to ask of each of us that he should be faithful to his own opportunities and make the most of his own blessings, without presuming to regulate the rest of the vast field.

WHAT MAKES A LIFE
SIGNIFICANT

WHAT MAKES A LIFE
SIGNIFICANT

IN my previous talk, 'On a Certain Blindness,' I tried to make you feel how soaked and shot-through life is with values and meanings which we fail to realize because of our external and insensible point of view. The meanings are there for the others, but they are not there for us. There lies more than a mere interest of curious speculation in understanding this. It has the most tremendous practical importance. I wish that I could convince you of it as I feel it myself. It is the basis of all our tolerance, social, religious, and political. The forgetting of it lies at the root of every stupid and sanguinary mistake that rulers over subject-peoples make. The first thing to learn in intercourse with others is non-interference with their own peculiar ways of being happy, provided those ways do not assume to interfere by violence with ours. No one has insight into all the ideals. No one should presume to judge them off-hand. The pretension to dogmatize about them in each other is the root of most human injustices and cruelties, and the trait in human character most likely to make the angels weep.

Every Jack sees in his own particular Jill charms and perfections to the enchantment of which we stolid onlookers are stone-cold. And which has the superior view of the absolute truth, he or we? Which has the more vital insight into the nature of Jill's existence, as a fact? Is he in excess, being in this matter a maniac? or are we in defect, being victims of a pathological anæsthesia as regards Jill's magical importance? Surely the latter; surely to Jack are the profounder truths revealed; surely poor Jill's palpitating little life-throbs *are* among the wonders of creation, *are* worthy of this sympathetic interest; and it is to our shame that the rest of us cannot feel like Jack. For Jack realizes Jill concretely, and we do not. He struggles toward a union with her inner life, divining her feelings, anticipating her desires, understanding her limits as manfully as he can, and yet inadequately, too; for he is also afflicted with some blindness, even here. Whilst we, dead clods that we are, do not even seek after these things, but are contented that that portion of eternal fact named Jill should be for us as if it were not. Jill, who knows her inner life, knows that Jack's way of taking it — so importantly — is the true and serious way; and she responds to the truth in him by taking him truly and seriously, too. May the ancient blindness never wrap its clouds about either of them again! Where would any of *us* be, were there no one willing to know us as we really are or ready to repay us for *our* insight by making recognizant return? We ought, all of us, to realize each other in this intense, pathetic, and important way.

If you say that this is absurd, and that we cannot be in love with everyone at once, I merely point out to you that, as a matter of fact, certain persons do exist with an enormous capacity for friendship and for taking delight in other people's lives; and that such persons know more of truth than if their hearts were not so big. The vice of ordinary Jack and Jill affection is not its intensity, but its exclusions and its jealousies. Leave those out, and you see that the ideal I am holding up before you, however impracticable to-day, yet contains nothing intrinsically absurd.

We have unquestionably a great cloud-bank of ancestral blindness weighing down upon us, only transiently riven here and there by fitful revelations of the truth. It is vain to hope for this state of things to alter much. Our inner secrets must remain for the most part impenetrable by others, for beings as essentially practical as we are are necessarily short of sight. But, if we cannot gain much positive insight into one another, cannot we at least use our sense of our own blindness to make us more cautious in going over the dark places? Cannot we escape some of those hideous ancestral intolerances and cruelties, and positive reversals of the truth?

For the remainder of this hour I invite you to seek with me some principle to make our tolerance less chaotic. And, as I began my previous lecture by a personal reminiscence, I am going to ask your indulgence for a similar bit of egotism now.

A few summers ago I spent a happy week at the famous Assembly Grounds on the borders of Chautauqua Lake. The moment one treads that sacred enclosure, one feels one's self in an atmosphere of success. Sobriety and industry, intelligence and goodness, orderliness and ideality, prosperity and cheerfulness, pervade the air. It is a serious and studious picnic on a gigantic scale. Here you have a town of many thousands of inhabitants, beautifully laid out in the forest and drained, and equipped with means for satisfying all the necessary lower and most of the superfluous higher wants of man. You have a first-class college in full blast. You have magnificent music — a chorus of seven hundred voices, with possibly the most perfect open-air auditorium in the world. You have every sort of athletic exercise from sailing, rowing, swimming, bicycling, to the ball-field and the more artificial doings which the gymnasium affords. You have kindergartens and model secondary schools. You have general religious services and special club-houses for the several sects. You have perpetually running soda-water fountains, and daily popular lectures by distinguished men. You have the best of company, and yet no effort. You have no zymotic diseases, no poverty, no drunkenness, no crime, no police. You have culture, you have kindness, you have cheapness, you have equality, you have the best fruits of what mankind has fought and bled and striven for under the name of civilization

for centuries. You have, in short, a fore-
taste of what human society might be, were
it all in the light, with no suffering and no
dark corners.

I went in curiosity for a day. I stayed
for a week, held spell-bound by the charm
and ease of everything, by the middle-class
paradise, without a sin, without a victim,
without a blot, without a tear.

And yet what was my own astonishment,
on emerging into the dark and wicked world
again, to catch myself quite unexpectedly
and involuntarily saying: "Ouf! what a
relief! Now for something primordial and
savage, even though it were as bad as an
Armenian massacre, to set the balance
straight again. This order is too tame, this
culture too second-rate, this goodness too
uninspiring. This human drama without a
villain or a pang; this community so refined
that ice-cream soda-water is the utmost
offering it can make to the brute animal
in man; this city simmering in the tepid
lakeside sun; this atrocious harmlessness

of all things, — I cannot abide with them. Let me take my chances again in the big outside worldly wilderness with all its sins and sufferings. There are the heights and depths, the precipices and the steep ideals, the gleams of the awful and the infinite; and there is more hope and help a thousand times than in this dead level and quintessence of every mediocrity."

Such was the sudden right-about-face performed for me by my lawless fancy! There had been spread before me the realization —on a small, sample scale of course —of all the ideals for which our civilization has been striving: security, intelligence, humanity, and order; and here was the instinctive hostile reaction, not of the natural man, but of a so-called cultivated man upon such a Utopia. There seemed thus to be a self-contradiction and paradox somewhere, which I, as a professor drawing a full salary, was in duty bound to unravel and explain, if I could.

So I meditated. And, first of all, I asked

myself what the thing was that was so lack-
ing in this Sabbatical city, and the lack of
which kept one forever falling short of the
higher sort of contentment. And I soon
recognized that it was the element that
gives to the wicked outer world all its moral
style, expressiveness, and picturesqueness,
— the element of precipitousness, so to call
it, of strength and strenuousness, intensity
and danger. What excites and interests
the looker-on at life, what the romances and
the statues celebrate and the grim civic
monuments remind us of, is the everlast-
ing battle of the powers of light with those
of darkness; with heroism, reduced to its
bare chance, yet ever and anon snatching
victory from the jaws of death. But in
this unspeakable Chautauqua there was no
potentiality of death in sight anywhere,
and no point of the compass visible from
which danger might possibly appear. The
ideal was so completely victorious already
that no sign of any previous battle re-
mained, the place just resting on its oars.

But what our human emotions seem to require is the sight of the struggle going on. The moment the fruits are being merely eaten, things become ignoble. Sweat and effort, human nature strained to its uttermost and on the rack, yet getting through alive, and then turning its back on its success to pursue another more rare and arduous still — this is the sort of thing the presence of which inspires us, and the reality of which it seems to be the function of all the higher forms of literature and fine art to bring home to us and suggest. At Chautauqua there were no racks, even in the place's historical museum; and no sweat, except possibly the gentle moisture on the brow of some lecturer, or on the sides of some player in the ball-field.

Such absence of human nature *in extremis* anywhere seemed, then, a sufficient explanation for Chautauqua's flatness and lack of zest.

But was not this a paradox well calculated to fill one with dismay? It looks indeed, thought I, as if the romantic idealists with their pessimism about our civilization were, after all, quite right. An irremediable flatness is coming over the world. Bourgeoisie and mediocrity, church sociables and teachers' conventions, are taking the place of the old heights and depths and romantic chiaroscuro. And, to get human life in its wild intensity, we must in future turn more and more away from the actual, and forget it, if we can, in the romancer's or the poet's pages. The whole world, delightful and sinful as it may still appear for a moment to one just escaped from the Chautauquan enclosure, is nevertheless obeying more and more just those ideals that are sure to make of it in the end a mere Chautauqua Assembly on an enormous scale. *Was im Gesang soll leben muss im Leben untergehn.* Even now, in our own country, correctness, fairness, and compromise for every small advantage are crowding out all other qualities. The higher

heroisms and the old rare flavors are passing out of life.[1]

With these thoughts in my mind, I was
speeding with the train toward Buffalo,
when, near that city, the sight of a workman
doing something on the dizzy edge of a
sky-scaling iron construction brought me
to my senses very suddenly. And now I
perceived, by a flash of insight, that I had
been steeping myself in pure ancestral
blindness, and looking at life with the eyes
of a remote spectator. Wishing for heroism
and the spectacle of human nature on the
rack, I had never noticed the great fields of
heroism lying round about me, I had failed
to see it present and alive. I could only
think of it as dead and embalmed, labelled
and costumed, as it is in the pages of romance. And yet there it was before me in
the daily lives of the laboring classes. Not
in clanging fights and desperate marches

[1] This address was composed before the Cuban and Philip-
pine wars. Such outbursts of the passion of mastery are, however, only episodes in a social process which in the long run seems
everywhere tending toward the Chautauquan ideals.

only is heroism to be looked for, but on every railway bridge and fire-proof building that is going up to-day. On freight-trains, on the decks of vessels, in cattle-yards and mines, on lumber-rafts, among the firemen and the policemen, the demand for courage is incessant; and the supply never fails. There, every day of the year somewhere, is human nature *in extremis* for you. And wherever a scythe, an axe, a pick, or a shovel is wielded, you have it sweating and aching and with its powers of patient endurance racked to the utmost under the length of hours of the strain.

As I awoke to all this unidealized heroic life around me, the scales seemed to fall from my eyes; and a wave of sympathy greater than anything I had ever before felt with the common life of common men began to fill my soul. It began to seem as if virtue with horny hands and dirty skin were the only virtue genuine and vital enough to take account of. Every other virtue poses; none is absolutely unconscious and simple, and unexpectant of decoration or recognition, like this. These are our soldiers, thought I, these our sustainers, these the very parents of our life.

Many years ago, when in Vienna, I had had a similar feeling of awe and reverence in looking at the peasant-women, in from the country on their business at the market for the day. Old hags many of them were, dried and brown and wrinkled, kerchiefed and short-petticoated, with thick wool stockings on their bony shanks, stumping through the glittering thoroughfares, looking neither to the right nor the left, bent on duty, envying nothing, humble-hearted, remote; — and yet at bottom, when you came to think of it, bearing the whole fabric of the splendors and corruptions of that city on their laborious backs. For where would any of it have been without their unremitting, unrewarded labor in the fields? And so with us: not to our generals and poets, I thought, but to the Italian and Hungarian laborers in the Subway, rather, ought the

monuments of gratitude and reverence of a
city like Boston to be reared.

If any of you have been readers of Tolstoï, you will see that I passed into a vein
of feeling similar to his, with its abhorrence
of all that conventionally passes for distinguished, and its exclusive deification of the
bravery, patience, kindliness, and dumbness
of the unconscious natural man.

Where now is *our* Tolstoï, I said, to bring
the truth of all this home to our American
bosoms, fill us with a better insight, and
wean us away from that spurious literary
romanticism on which our wretched culture
—as it calls itself—is fed? Divinity lies
all about us, and culture is too hidebound
to even suspect the fact. Could a Howells
or a Kipling be enlisted in this mission?
or are they still too deep in the ancestral
blindness, and not humane enough for the
inner joy and meaning of the laborer's
existence to be really revealed? Must we
wait for some one born and bred and living

as a laborer himself, but who, by grace of Heaven, shall also find a literary voice?

And there I rested on that day, with a sense of widening of vision, and with what it is surely fair to call an increase of religious insight into life. In God's eyes the differences of social position, of intellect, of culture, of cleanliness, of dress, which different men exhibit, and all the other rarities and exceptions on which they so fantastically pin their pride, must be so small as practically quite to vanish; and all that should remain is the common fact that here we are, a countless multitude of vessels of life, each of us pent in to peculiar difficulties, with which we must severally struggle by using whatever of fortitude and goodness we can summon up. The exercise of the courage, patience, and kindness, must be the significant portion of the whole business; and the distinctions of position can only be a matter of diversifying the phenomenal surface upon which these underground virtues may manifest their effects. At this rate, the deepest human life is everywhere, is eternal. And, if any human attributes exist only in particular individuals, they must belong to the mere trapping and decoration of the surface-show.

Thus are men's lives levelled up as well as levelled down, — levelled up in their common inner meaning, levelled down in their outer gloriousness and show. Yet always, we must confess, this levelling insight tends to be obscured again; and always the ancestral blindness returns and wraps us up, so that we end once more by thinking that creation can be for no other purpose than to develop remarkable situations and conventional distinctions and merits. And then always some new leveller in the shape of a religious prophet has to arise — the Buddha, the Christ, or some Saint Francis, some Rousseau or Tolstoï — to redispel our blindness. Yet, little by little, there comes some stable gain; for the world does get more humane, and the religion of democracy tends toward permanent increase.

This, as I said, became for a time my conviction, and gave me great content. I have put the matter into the form of a personal reminiscence, so that I might lead you into it more directly and completely, and so save time. But now I am going to discuss the rest of it with you in a more impersonal way.

Tolstoï's levelling philosophy began long before he had the crisis of melancholy commemorated in that wonderful document of his entitled 'My Confession,' which led the way to his more specifically religious works. In his masterpiece 'War and Peace,' — assuredly the greatest of human novels, — the rôle of the spiritual hero is given to a poor little soldier named Karataïeff, so helpful, so cheerful, and so devout that, in spite of his ignorance and filthiness, the sight of him opens the heavens, which have been closed, to the mind of the principal character of the book; and his example evidently is meant by Tolstoï to let God into the world again for the reader.

Poor little Karataïeff is taken prisoner by the French; and, when too exhausted by hardship and fever to march, is shot as other prisoners were in the famous retreat from Moscow. The last view one gets of him is his little figure leaning against a white birch-tree, and uncomplainingly awaiting the end.

"The more," writes Tolstoï in the work 'My Confession,' "the more I examined the life of these laboring folks, the more persuaded I became that they veritably have faith, and get from it alone the sense and the possibility of life. . . . Contrariwise to those of our own class, who protest against destiny and grow indignant at its rigor, these people receive maladies and misfortunes without revolt, without opposition, and with a firm and tranquil confidence that all had to be like that, could not be otherwise, and that it is all right so. . . . The more we live by our intellect, the less we understand the meaning of life. We see only a cruel jest in suffering and death, whereas these people live, suffer, and draw near to death with tranquillity, and oftener than not with joy. . . . There are enormous multitudes of them happy with the most perfect happiness, although deprived of what for us is the sole good of life. Those who understand life's meaning, and know how to live and die thus, are to be counted not by twos, threes, tens, but by hundreds, thousands, millions. They labor quietly, endure privations and pains, live and die, and throughout everything see the good without seeing the vanity. I had to love these people. The more I entered into their life, the more I loved them; and the more it became possible for me to live, too. It came about not only that the life of our society, of the learned and of the rich, disgusted me — more than that, it lost all semblance of meaning in my eyes. All our actions, our deliberations, our sciences, our arts, all appeared to me with a new significance. I understood that these things might be charming pastimes, but that one need seek in them no depth, whereas the life of the hard-working populace, of that multitude of human beings who really contribute to existence, appeared to me in its true light. I understood that there veritably is life, that the meaning which life there receives is the truth; and I accepted it." [1]

In a similar way does Stevenson appeal to our piety toward the elemental virtue of mankind.

"What a wonderful thing," he writes,[2] "is this Man! How surprising are his attributes! Poor soul, here for so little, cast among so many hardships, savagely surrounded, savagely descended, irremediably condemned to prey upon his fellow-lives, —who should have blamed him, had he been of a piece with his destiny and a being merely barbarous? . . . [Yet] it matters not where we look, under what climate we observe him, in what stage of society,

[1] My Confession, X. (condensed).
[2] Across the Plains: 'Pulvis et Umbra' (abridged).

in what depth of ignorance, burdened with
what erroneous morality; in ships at sea,
a man inured to hardship and vile pleasures, his brightest hope a fiddle in a tavern,
and a bedizened trull who sells herself to
rob him, and he, for all that, simple, inno-
cent, cheerful, kindly like a child, constant
to toil, brave to drown, for others; . . .
in the slums of cities, moving among indif-
ferent millions to mechanical employments,
without hope of change in the future, with
scarce a pleasure in the present, and yet
true to his virtues, honest up to his lights,
kind to his neighbors, tempted perhaps in
vain by the bright gin-palace, . . . often
repaying the world's scorn with service,
often standing firm upon a scruple; . . .
everywhere some virtue cherished or affected,
everywhere some decency of thought and
courage, everywhere the ensign of man's
ineffectual goodness, — ah! if I could show
you this! If I could show you these men
and women all the world over, in every stage
of history, under every abuse of error,

under every circumstance of failure, without hope, without help, without thanks, still obscurely fighting the last fight of virtue, still clinging to some rag of honor, the poor jewel of their souls."

All this is as true as it is splendid, and terribly do we need our Tolstoïs and Stevensons to keep our sense for it alive. Yet you remember the Irishman who, when asked, "Is not one man as good as another?" replied, "Yes; and a great deal better, too!" Similarly (it seems to me) does Tolstoï overcorrect our social prejudices, when he makes his love of the peasant so exclusive, and hardens his heart toward the educated man as absolutely as he does. Grant that at Chautauqua there was little moral effort, little sweat or muscular strain in view. Still, deep down in the souls of the participants we may be sure that something of the sort was hid, some inner stress, some vital virtue not found wanting when required. And, after all, the question recurs, and forces itself upon us, Is it so certain that the surroundings and circumstances of the virtue do make so little difference in the importance of the result? Is the functional utility, the worth to the universe of a certain definite amount of courage, kindliness, and patience, no greater if the possessor of these virtues is in an educated situation, working out far-reaching tasks, than if he be an illiterate nobody, hewing wood and drawing water, just to keep himself alive? Tolstoï's philosophy, deeply enlightening though it certainly is, remains a false abstraction. It savors too much of that Oriental pessimism and nihilism of his, which declares the whole phenomenal world and its facts and their distinctions to be a cunning fraud.

A mere bare fraud is just what our Western common sense will never believe the phenomenal world to be. It admits fully that the inner joys and virtues are the *essential* part of life's business, but it is sure that *some* positive part is also played by the adjuncts of the show. If it is idiotic in romanticism to recognize the heroic only when it sees it labelled and dressed-up in books, it is really just as idiotic to see it only in the dirty boots and sweaty shirt of some one in the fields. It is with us really under every disguise: at Chautauqua; here in your college; in the stock-yards and on the freight-trains; and in the czar of Russia's court. But, instinctively, we make a combination of two things in judging the total significance of a human being. We feel it to be some sort of a product (if such a product only could be calculated) of his inner virtue *and* his outer place, —neither singly taken, but both conjoined. If the outer differences had no meaning for life, why indeed should all this immense variety of them exist? They *must* be significant elements of the world as well.

Just test Tolstoï's deification of the mere manual laborer by the facts. This is what Mr. Walter Wyckoff, after working as an unskilled laborer in the demolition of some buildings at West Point, writes of the spiritual condition of the class of men to which he temporarily chose to belong:—

"The salient features of our condition are plain enough. We are grown men, and are without a trade. In the labor-market we stand ready to sell to the highest bidder our mere muscular strength for so many hours each day. We are thus in the lowest grade of labor. And, selling our muscular strength in the open market for what it will bring, we sell it under peculiar conditions. It is all the capital that we have. We have no reserve means of subsistence, and cannot, therefore, stand off for a 'reserve price.' We sell under the necessity of satisfying imminent hunger. Broadly speaking, we must sell our labor or starve; and, as hunger is a matter of a few hours, and we have no other way of meeting this need, we must sell at once for what the market offers for our labor.

"Our employer is buying labor in a dear market, and he will certainly get from us as much work as he can at the price. The gang-boss is secured for this purpose, and thoroughly does he know his business. He has sole command of us. He never saw us before, and he will discharge us all when the débris is cleared away. In the meantime he must get from us, if he can, the utmost of physical labor which we, individually and collectively, are capable of. If he should drive some of us to exhaustion, and we should not be able to continue at work, he would not be the loser; for the market would soon supply him with others to take our places.

"We are ignorant men, but so much we clearly see, — that we have sold our labor where we could sell it dearest, and our employer has bought it where he could buy it cheapest. He has paid high, and he must get all the labor that he can; and, by a strong instinct which possesses us, we shall part with as little as we can. From work like ours there seems to us to have been eliminated every element which constitutes the nobility of labor. We feel no personal pride in its progress, and no community of interest with our employer. There is none of the joy of responsibility, none of the sense of achievement, only the dull monotony of grinding toil, with the longing for the signal to quit work, and for our wages at the end.

"And being what we are, the dregs of the labor-market, and having no certainty of permanent employment, and no organization among ourselves, we must expect to work under the watchful eye of a gang-boss, and be driven, like the wage-slaves that we are, through our tasks.

"All this is to tell us, in effect, that our lives are hard, barren, hopeless lives."

And such hard, barren, hopeless lives, surely, are not lives in which one ought to be willing permanently to remain. And why is this so? Is it because they are so dirty? Well, Nansen grew a great deal dirtier on his polar expedition; and we think none the worse of his life for that. Is it the insensibility? Our soldiers have to grow vastly more insensible, and we extol them to the skies. Is it the poverty? Poverty has been reckoned the crowning beauty of many a heroic career. Is it the slavery to a task, the loss of finer pleasures? Such slavery and loss are of the very essence of the higher fortitude, and are always counted to its credit, — read the records of missionary devotion all over the world. It is not any one of these things, then, taken by itself, — no, nor all of them together, — that make such a life undesirable. A man might in truth live like an unskilled laborer, and do the work of one, and yet count as one of the noblest of God's creatures. Quite possibly there were some such persons in the gang that our author describes; but the current of their souls ran underground; and he was too steeped in the ancestral blindness to discern it.

If there *were* any such morally exceptional individuals, however, what made them different from the rest? It can only have been this, — that their souls worked and endured in obedience to some inner *ideal*, while their comrades were not actuated by anything worthy of that name. These ideals of other lives are among those secrets that we can almost never penetrate, although something about the man may often tell us when they are there. In Mr. Wyckoff's own case we know exactly what the self-imposed ideal was. Partly he had stumped himself, as the boys say, to carry through a strenuous achievement; but mainly he wished to enlarge his sympathetic insight into fellow-lives. For this his sweat and toil acquire a certain heroic significance, and make us accord to him exceptional esteem. But it is easy to imagine his fellows with various other ideals. To say nothing of wives and babies, one may have been a convert of the Salvation Army, and had a nightingale singing of expiation and forgiveness in his heart all the while he labored. Or there might have been an apostle like Tolstoï himself, or his compatriot Bondareff, in the gang, voluntarily embracing labor as their religious mission. Class-loyalty was undoubtedly an ideal with many. And who knows how much of that higher manliness of poverty, of which Phillips Brooks has spoken so penetratingly, was or was not present in that gang?

"A rugged, barren land," says Phillips Brooks, "is poverty to live in, — a land where I am thankful very often if I can get a berry or a root to eat. But living in it really, letting it bear witness to me of itself, not dishonoring it all the time by judging it after the standard of the other lands, gradually there come out its qualities. Behold! no land like this barren and naked land of poverty could show the moral geology of the world. See how the hard ribs . . . stand out strong and solid. No life like poverty could so get one to the heart of things and make men know their meaning, could so let us feel life and the world with all the soft cushions stripped off and thrown away. . . . Poverty makes men come very near each other, and recognize each other's human hearts; and poverty, highest and best of all, demands and cries out for faith in God. . . . I know how super-ficial and unfeeling, how like mere mockery, words in praise of poverty may seem. . . . But I am sure that the poor man's dignity and freedom, his self-respect and energy, depend upon his cordial knowledge that his poverty is a true region and kind of life, with its own chances of character, its own springs of happiness and revelations of God. Let him resist the characterless-ness which often goes with being poor. Let him insist on respecting the condition where he lives. Let him learn to love it, so that by and by, [if] he grows rich, he shall go out of the low door of the old familiar poverty with a true pang of regret, and with a true honor for the narrow home in which he has lived so long." [1]

The barrenness and ignobleness of the more usual laborer's life consist in the fact

[1] Sermons, 5th Series, New York, 1893, pp. 166, 167.

that it is moved by no such ideal inner springs. The backache, the long hours, the danger, are patiently endured — for what? To gain a quid of tobacco, a glass of beer, a cup of coffee, a meal, and a bed, and to begin again the next day and shirk as much as one can. This really is why we raise no monument to the laborers in the Subway, even though they be our conscripts, and even though after a fashion our city is indeed based upon their patient hearts and enduring backs and shoulders. And this is why we do raise monuments to our soldiers, whose outward conditions were even brutaller still. The soldiers are supposed to have followed an ideal, and the laborers are supposed to have followed none.

You see, my friends, how the plot now thickens; and how strangely the complexities of this wonderful human nature of ours begin to develop under our hands. We have seen the blindness and deadness to each other which are our natural inheritance;

and, in spite of them, we have been led to acknowledge an inner meaning which passeth show, and which may be present in the lives of others where we least descry it. And now we are led to say that such inner meaning can be *complete* and *valid for us also*, only when the inner joy, courage, and endurance are joined with an ideal.

But what, exactly, do we mean by an ideal? Can we give no definite account of such a word?

To a certain extent we can. An ideal, for instance, must be something intellectually conceived, something of which we are not unconscious, if we have it; and it must carry with it that sort of outlook, uplift, and brightness that go with all intellectual facts. Secondly, there must be *novelty* in an ideal, — novelty at least for him whom the ideal grasps. Sodden routine is incompatible with ideality, although what is sodden routine for one person may be ideal novelty for another. This shows

that there is nothing absolutely ideal: ideals
are relative to the lives that entertain them.
To keep out of the gutter is for us here no
part of consciousness at all, yet for many of
our brethren it is the most legitimately
engrossing of ideals.

Now, taken nakedly, abstractly, and im-
mediately, you see that mere ideals are the
cheapest things in life. Everybody has
them in some shape or other, personal
or general, sound or mistaken, low or high;
and the most worthless sentimentalists and
dreamers, drunkards, shirks and verse-
makers, who never show a grain of effort,
courage, or endurance, possibly have them
on the most copious scale. Education,
enlarging as it does our horizon and perspective, is a means of multiplying our ideals,
of bringing new ones into view. And your
college professor, with a starched shirt and
spectacles, would, if a stock of ideals were
all alone by itself enough to render a life
significant, be the most absolutely and deeply
significant of men. Tolstoï would be com-

pletely blind in despising him for a prig, a pedant, and a parody; and all our new insight into the divinity of muscular labor would be altogether off the track of truth.

But such consequences as this, you instinctively feel, are erroneous. The more ideals a man has, the more contemptible, on the whole, do you continue to deem him, if the matter ends there for him, and if none of the laboring man's virtues are called into action on his part, — no courage shown, no privations undergone, no dirt or scars contracted in the attempt to get them realized. It is quite obvious that something more than the mere possession of ideals is required to make a life significant in any sense that claims the spectator's admiration. Inner joy, to be sure, it may *have*, with its ideals; but that is its own private sentimental matter. To extort from us, outsiders as we are, with our own ideals to look after, the tribute of our grudging recognition, it must back its ideal visions with what the laborers have, the sterner stuff of manly virtue; it must multiply their sentimental surface by the dimension of the active will, if we are to have *depth*, if we are to have anything cubical and solid in the way of character.

The significance of a human life for communicable and publicly recognizable purposes is thus the offspring of a marriage of two different parents, either of whom alone is barren. The ideals taken by themselves give no reality, the virtues by themselves no novelty. And let the orientalists and pessimists say what they will, the thing of deepest — or, at any rate, of comparatively deepest — significance in life does seem to be its character of *progress*, or that strange union of reality with ideal novelty which it continues from one moment to another to present. To recognize ideal novelty is the task of what we call intelligence. Not everyone's intelligence can tell which novelties are ideal. For many the ideal thing will always seem to cling still to the older more familiar good. In this case character, though not significant totally, may be still significant pathetically. So, if we are to choose which is the more essential factor of human character, the fighting virtue or the intellectual breadth, we must side with Tolstoï, and choose that simple faithfulness to his light or darkness which any common unintellectual man can show.

But, with all this beating and tacking on my part, I fear you take me to be reaching a confused result. I seem to be just taking things up and dropping them again. First I took up Chautauqua, and dropped that; then Tolstoï, and the heroism of common toil, and dropped them; finally, I took up ideals, and seem now almost dropping those. But please observe in what sense it is that I drop them. It is when they pretend *singly* to redeem life from insignificance. Culture and refinement all alone are not enough to do so. Ideal aspirations are not enough, when uncombined with pluck and will. But neither are pluck and will, dogged endurance and insensibility to danger enough, when taken all alone. There must be some sort of fusion, some chemical combination among these principles, for a life objectively and thoroughly significant to result.

Of course, this is a somewhat vague conclusion. But in a question of significance, of worth, like this, conclusions can never be precise. The answer of appreciation, of sentiment, is always a more or a less, a balance struck by sympathy, insight, and good will. But it is an answer, all the same, a real conclusion. And, in the course of getting it, it seems to me that our eyes have been opened to many important things. Some of you are, perhaps, more livingly aware than you were an hour ago of the depths of worth that lie around you, hid in alien lives. And, when you ask how much sympathy you ought to bestow, although the amount is, truly enough, a matter of ideal on your own part, yet in this notion of the combination of ideals with active virtues you have a rough standard for shaping your decision. In any case, your imagination is extended. You divine in the world about you matter for a little more humility on your own part, and tolerance, reverence, and love for others; and you gain a certain inner joyfulness at the increased importance of our common life. Such joyfulness is a religious inspiration and an element of spiritual health, and worth more than large amounts of that sort of technical and accurate information which we professors are supposed to be able to impart.

To show the sort of thing I mean by these words, I will just make one brief practical illustration, and then close.

We are suffering to-day in America from what is called the labor-question; and, when you go out into the world, you will each and all of you be caught up in its perplexities. I use the brief term labor-question to cover all sorts of anarchistic discontents and socialistic projects, and the conservative

resistances which they provoke. So far as
this conflict is unhealthy and regrettable,
— and I think it is so only to a limited
extent, — the unhealthiness consists solely
in the fact that one-half of our fellow-coun-
trymen remain entirely blind to the internal
significance of the lives of the other half.
They miss the joys and sorrows, they fail
to feel the moral virtue, and they do not
guess the presence of the intellectual ideals.
They are at cross-purposes all along the line,
regarding each other as they might regard
a set of dangerously gesticulating automata,
or, if they seek to get at the inner motiva-
tion, making the most horrible mistakes.
Often all that the poor man can think of
in the rich man is a cowardly greediness
for safety, luxury, and effeminacy, and a
boundless affectation. What he is, is not
a human being, but a pocket-book, a bank-
account. And a similar greediness, turned
by disappointment into envy, is all that
many rich men can see in the state of mind
of the dissatisfied poor. And, if the rich

man begins to do the sentimental act over the poor man, what senseless blunders does he make, pitying him for just those very duties and those very immunities which, rightly taken, are the condition of his most abiding and characteristic joys! Each, in short, ignores the fact that happiness and unhappiness and significance are a vital mystery; each pins them absolutely on some ridiculous feature of the external situation; and everybody remains outside of everybody else's sight.

Society has, with all this, undoubtedly got to pass toward some newer and better equilibrium, and the distribution of wealth has doubtless slowly got to change: such changes have always happened, and will happen to the end of time. But if, after all that I have said, any of you expect that they will make any *genuine vital difference* on a large scale, to the lives of our descendants, you will have missed the significance of my entire lecture. The solid meaning of life is always the same eternal

thing, — the marriage, namely, of some
unhabitual ideal, however special, with
some fidelity, courage, and endurance; with
some man's or woman's pains. — And, whatever or wherever life may be, there will
always be the chance for that marriage to
take place.

Fitz-James Stephen wrote many years
ago words to this effect more eloquent than
any I can speak: "The 'Great Eastern,' or
some of her successors," he said, "will perhaps defy the roll of the Atlantic, and cross
the seas without allowing their passengers
to feel that they have left the firm land.
The voyage from the cradle to the grave
may come to be performed with similar
facility. Progress and science may perhaps
enable untold millions to live and die without a care, without a pang, without an
anxiety. They will have a pleasant passage and plenty of brilliant conversation.
They will wonder that men ever believed
at all in clanging fights and blazing towns
and sinking ships and praying hands; and,

when they come to the end of their course, they will go their way, and the place thereof will know them no more. But it seems unlikely that they will have such a knowledge of the great ocean on which they sail, with its storms and wrecks, its currents and icebergs, its huge waves and mighty winds, as those who battled with it for years together in the little craft, which, if they had few other merits, brought those who navigated them full into the presence of time and eternity, their maker and themselves, and forced them to have some definite view of their relations to them and to each other." [1]

In this solid and tridimensional sense, so to call it, those philosophers are right who contend that the world is a standing thing, with no progress, no real history. The changing conditions of history touch only the surface of the show. The altered equilibriums and redistributions only diversify our opportunities and open chances to us

[1] Essays by a Barrister, London, 1862, p. 318.

for new ideals. But, with each new ideal that comes into life, the chance for a life based on some old ideal will vanish; and he would needs be a presumptuous calculator who should with confidence say that the total sum of significances is positively and absolutely greater at any one epoch than at any other of the world.

I am speaking broadly, I know, and omitting to consider certain qualifications in which I myself believe. But one can only make one point in one lecture, and I shall be well content if I have brought my point home to you this evening in even a slight degree. *There are compensations:* and no outward changes of condition in life can keep the nightingale of its eternal meaning from singing in all sorts of different men's hearts. That is the main fact to remember. If we could not only admit it with our lips, but really and truly believe it, how our convulsive insistencies, how our antipathies and dreads of each other, would soften down! If the poor and the rich could look at each other in this way, *sub specie æternitatis*, how gentle would grow their disputes! what tolerance and good humor, what willingness to live and let live, would come into the world!

THE END

Made in the USA
Columbia, SC
14 November 2020